SHEEP, GOATS, AND WOLVES

Mark T. Barclay

All scripture references are quoted from the
King James Version of the Holy Bible
unless otherwise noted.

First Printing 1994

ISBN 0-944802-06-0

Write:
Mark Barclay Ministries
P.O. Box 588, Midland, MI 48640-0588

CONTENTS

INTRODUCTION

SHEEP - GOATS - WOLVES

Many times in the public ministry of Jesus Christ we see that He used figurative speech such as parables and allegories. He was so simple in His speech and delivery that most men marveled. He had a way of transferring truth from His heart to others by means of familiar illustrations and surroundings.

For example, Jesus, while selecting and gathering His original 12 disciples, found some of them to be fishermen. In His expertise of communication, He addressed them and lured them through terms they would relate to. He said to them (as they were fishing in the Sea of Galilee), "Come, follow me, and I will make you fishers of men."

Certainly these men didn't know all the details of catching men, but they could relate because they knew the principles of fishing and the lifestyle of a fisherman.

Many times in the Scriptures we see authors using this form of communication. I find that there are certain comparisons and substitutions used more often than others. For example, the terms sheep, shepherds, herds, goats, flocks, and wolves are used very often in both the Old and New

Testaments by our Lord Jesus and writers like Paul, James, Peter, and John. Perhaps this is due to the way of livelihood found in the Middle East. There are many flocks and herds roaming with shepherds or herdsman (I suppose even more so in the years past).

Because this way of communication is so easy to read and understand and because it truly does relate to us today, I have chosen to follow this theme throughout this book— *Sheep, Goats, and Wolves*.

I will be expounding scriptures and sharing experiences in human behavior by means of figurative speech and trying to cause you, the reader, to picture in your mind the life of the shepherd with his sheep.

The spiritual application, as you will see, comes to us as we examine our local church congregations (flocks) which consist of obedient Christians (sheep); those who agitate and cause turmoil (goats); those who are yet carnal, causing division, strife, and schism (wolves); and the pastors of these churches (shepherds).

A WORD FROM THE AUTHOR

The intention of the author is to enlighten all church members of the various degrees of human relationships and behavior patterns found in our congregations. Each reader will be self-quizzed as he discovers the message on the pages of this book. The questions that will arise are: Am I an obedient sheep? Am I a goat, always agitating and not quite obedient? Am I a wolf, dividing and destroying the well-being of the flock of God?

Of course, every one of us wants to be a good little sheep!

It is the desire of the author that each pastor who reads this book would be better equipped and also encouraged in dealing with his flock and in handling hard situations. It is also the motivation of the author to expose the sly, deceitful activity of the enemy in our local church families and, in doing so, destroy his stronghold on so many of God's people.

In reading these pages that follow, pastors will get a better understanding of the different kinds of people they are dealing with and, of course, how to deal with each.

I take a moment here as I write this book to pray for you. I pray that the Great Teacher, the Holy Spirit, will open your hearts to the truths that lie on these pages. I pray that you will read and examine this book with humility and holiness, being willing to admit what and who you are and make steps to change for the better.

I invite you to read this book and enjoy its style, content, and meaning. However, I give you a fair and friendly warning—you will not enjoy this book if you are in strife, backslidden, bitter, or full of anxiety or if you are in opposition to church leadership or your heart isn't right with God.

I write this book in love and humility with hopes that it will better the body of Christ and cause us to be more strongly knit together.

CHAPTER 1
THE SCRIPTURES

"The fool hath said in his heart, There is no God . . ."

Psalm 14:1

". . . Believe in the LORD *your God, so shall ye be established; believe his prophets, so shall ye prosper."*

2 Chronicles 20:20

"All scripture is given by inspiration of God, and is profitable for doctrine, for reproof, for correction, for instruction in righteousness:

That the man of God may be perfect, thoroughly furnished unto all good works."

2 Timothy 3:16-17

"Preach the word; be instant in season, out of season; reprove, rebuke, exhort with all long-suffering and doctrine.

For the time will come when they will not endure sound doctrine; but after their own lusts shall they heap to themselves teachers, having itching ears;

And they shall turn away their ears from the truth, and shall be turned unto fables.

But watch thou in all things, endure afflictions, do the

1

work of an evangelist, make full proof of thy ministry."

2 Timothy 4:2-5

". . . Woe be to the shepherds of Israel that do feed themselves! should not the shepherds feed the flocks?

Ye eat the fat, and ye clothe you with the wool, ye kill them that are fed: but ye feed not the flock.

The diseased have ye not strengthened, neither have ye healed that which was sick, neither have ye bound up that which was broken, neither have ye brought again that which was driven away, neither have ye sought that which was lost; but with force and with cruelty have ye ruled them.

And they were scattered, because there is no shepherd: and they became meat to all the beasts of the field, when they were scattered.

My sheep wandered through all the mountains, and upon every high hill: yea, my flock was scattered upon all the face of the earth, and none did search or seek after them."

Ezekiel 34:2-6

"As a shepherd seeketh out his flock in the day that he is among his sheep that are scattered; so will I seek out my sheep, and will deliver them out of all places where they have been scattered in the cloudy and dark day.

And I will bring them out from the people, and gather them from the countries, and will bring them to their own land, and feed them upon the mountains of Israel by the rivers, and in all the inhabited places of the country.

I will feed them in a good pasture, and upon the high

mountains of Israel shall their fold be: there shall they lie in a good fold, and in a fat pasture shall they feed upon the mountains of Israel.

I will feed my flock, and I will cause them to lie down, saith the LORD GOD."

Ezekiel 34:12-15

"And I will give you pastors according to mine heart, which shall feed you with knowledge and understanding."

Jeremiah 3:15

"And Jehoash did that which was right in the sight of the LORD all his days wherein Jehoiada the priest instructed him."

2 Kings 12:2

"The LORD is my shepherd; I shall not want.

He maketh me to lie down in green pastures: he leadeth me beside the still waters."

Psalm 23:1-2

"For he is our God; and we are the people of his pasture, and the sheep of his hand . . ."

Psalm 95:7

"Be thou diligent to know the state of thy flocks, and look well to thy herds."

Proverbs 27:23

"The lambs are for thy clothing, and the goats are the price of the fields.

And thou shalt have goats' milk enough for thy food, for the food of thy household, and for the maintenance for thy maidens."

Proverbs 27:26-27

"Beware of false prophets, which come to you in sheep's clothing, but inwardly they are ravening wolves."

Matthew 7:15

"And before him shall be gathered all nations: and he shall separate them one from another, as a shepherd divideth his sheep from the goats:

And he shall set the sheep on his right hand, but the goats on the left."

Matthew 25:32-33

"I am the good shepherd: the good shepherd giveth his life for the sheep.

But he that is an hireling, and not the shepherd, whose own the sheep are not, seeth the wolf coming, and leaveth the sheep, and fleeth: and the wolf catcheth them, and scattereth the sheep."

John 10:11-12

"Take heed therefore unto yourselves, and to all the flock, over the which the Holy Ghost hath made you overseers, to feed the church of God, which he hath purchased with his own blood.

For I know this, that after my departing shall grievous wolves enter in among you, not sparing the flock.

Also of your own selves shall men arise, speaking perverse things, to draw away disciples after them."

Acts 20:28-30

"The elders which are among you I exhort.

Feed the flock of God which is among you, taking the oversight thereof, not by constraint, but willingly; not for filthy lucre, but of a ready mind;

Neither as being lords over God's heritage, but being ensamples to the flock.

And when the chief Shepherd shall appear, ye shall receive a crown of glory that fadeth not away."

1 Peter 5:1-4

"Obey them that have the rule over you, and submit yourselves: for they watch for your souls, as they that must give account, that they may do it with joy, and not with grief: for that is unprofitable for you."

Hebrews 13:17

CHAPTER 2
CHRISTIANS—NOT ALL THE SAME

I have observed that some people think all Christians are totally equal and exactly the same, and I suppose to a degree this is true. However, it doesn't take long to see differences when you look at each believer's assets (experiences, accomplishments, positions, anointing, and godly appointments) and calculate them with their deficits (hurts, failures, shipwrecks, temptations, sins, weights, and faith breaks).

Each believer should be serving God in his own capacity according to the measure that has been given him. Also, we have to remember there are different degrees in which these believers serve; i.e., some thirtyfold, some sixtyfold, some one hundredfold.

I have had the privilege of sharing the Lord in most of the states in America and in many foreign countries. I have learned many things and obtained a diversity of experiences. Out of these learning experiences, I have come to some simple conclusions about the kingdom of God in its relationship to this world.

People come in different sizes, colors, and shapes. They live in different climates and conditions, and they speak different languages. Temperatures vary as well as environment, weather, laws, and customs. But God is God everywhere! His Word works everywhere! The devil is the devil everywhere. Sin is sin everywhere, and strife is strife everywhere. There are certain principles and laws that do not change no matter where you go.

I always like to remind people that the Bible is the absolute, infallible, inspired Word of God no matter where it is read, spoken, or applied. Some people actually think they add validity to the Word of God by believing in it or that they take away from its validity by not believing in it. Let me tell you, the Word of God is the truth already settled in Heaven, and whether or not you believe it has absolutely no bearing at all. It is the truth. God is not a man that He should lie. The more you believe and confess it, the more it will work for you. Nevertheless, it is still the Word of God—believe it or not.

> *"All scripture is given by inspiration of God, and is profitable for doctrine, for reproof, for correction, for instruction in righteousness . . ."*
>
> 2 Timothy 3:16

A GOOD SHEPHERD

NEVER RUNS

WHEN THE WOLVES COME,

BUT HE FIGHTS

FOR HIS SHEEP.

CHAPTER 3
PASTORS—PEOPLE EXPERTS

In dealing with congregations as a Christian leader, I am constantly having to remind them that God has set in the church different ministries, administrations, and operations. There are many who don't see the separation in these things. Many can't even understand that God set some in the church as leaders and some as helpers. Some lead and govern. Some follow and help.

As I travel from church to church, I like to remind congregations that their pastor has a small advantage over them. He has been both a shepherd and a sheep.

The average Christian knows what it is to be a lamb or a sheep, but very few of them have ever been given a pastor's heart and appointment. However, every pastor has lived on both sides of the fence. He has been a member of the congregation and also a member of the pastorate. He knows what it's like to sit under pastoral leadership, and he knows what it's like to *be* that leadership. No pastor was born a pastor. Most pastors still remember what it is like to be in the sheepfold; therefore, they can still accurately understand and relate to the sheep.

This dual view of the Kingdom does not belong to

every believer because they only have experienced one side of the fence—sheep to shepherd. The average Christian has no idea what it is like to carry the load of pastoral responsibility; therefore, they need to be taught how to relate. Because most of them have never been a pastor, they can't rely on their memory or experience of the pastorate to help them relate.

Don't ever say your pastor doesn't understand, can't relate, or doesn't know what it is like.

Pastors are people experts! A man who has been set in the office of pastor by God will have a pastor's heart (see Jeremiah 3:15). Because he has God's heart, he begins to respond to people and their problems as God would. God created humanity; therefore, He is the highest authority on the provision, study, and behavior of humanity. If He puts His heart in a man and calls him a pastor, then that man becomes keen and wise to the details and elements of people.

I like to illustrate it this way. If you have a severe heart problem, you will go see a heart specialist for advice, medication, and perhaps even surgery. You wouldn't dream of allowing your best friend to work on your heart with his pocketknife—not even if he read two books and listened to several tapes on the subject or even if he graduated from a nine-month, super-cram course! It's your only heart, and you want to live, so you want a specialist—an expert. I buy insurance from my insurance agent because he not only is well-educated in the subject but also experienced. That is all he does day after day after day. So is it with my auto mechanic, my financial accountant, my doctor, my dentist, and so on.

Why is it we can allow all of these *licensed*, well-trained, and highly-experienced professionals to operate so well in their offices and submit ourselves to them so completely? Yet when it comes to pastors and the church, it's a free-for-all?

Don't you realize that a pastor has been educated and has studied hard to be a pastor? Don't you understand that he is *licensed* to do what he is doing? Don't you know God has set *some* in the church as leaders? Don't you realize that all your pastor does every day is work on people and their problems? He is an expert at it!

Sure you may have read some of the books he has read. Sure you may have listened to the same tapes he has listened to. Yes, I know you have prayed for some and counseled others. Of course you know the Scriptures and you've been to church. Sure your pastor serves the same God you do. You see, we are talking about the difference of a well-trained, experienced, approved, and licensed technician compared to a backyard mechanic. One has the right tools, manuals, proper conditions, know-how, experience, and parts, while the other works under the much lesser conditions with cheaper tools and not-quite-so-precise results. Somewhere near you is one of the best auto mechanics in your city, but if all your car ever sees is your garage, it's deprived. So is it with your soul.

I believe it's fair to say that God wants all of us to be sheep. He wishes that none would perish but that all would come to repentance. He sent His only begotten Son for the world, not just to a select few. Even realizing this, we know that some have not yet responded, some have left the fold, some have gone shipwreck in the faith, and so on. The result, of course, is that not all are good little lambs. There are also goats and wolves in our pastures and among our flocks.

Anybody knows you can't handle or relate to a sheep the same way you do a wolf. There are different ways to communicate to and respond to these different beings.

If a church family is relating to everyone exactly the same, then they are confused over goats, entertaining wolves, and probably abusing the sheep. This, of course, is also true with our Christian leaders. We must learn to know the difference between sheep, goats, and wolves and be able to deal with each accordingly.

Let me illustrate:

The body of Christ went through a season of over-attention to the devil. We began to say that everything that caused ungodly results in our lives was a demon or spirit. We began to have deliverance services, and the demons got more attention than God. Much of the time the people were not getting delivered but confused.

Now understand that there are demons, and there is legitimate deliverance in the blood of the Lamb. At the same time, there is a lot of foolishness and immaturity. Many people who had problems would go to get help. The "helpers" weren't able, most of the time, to discern between flesh and spirit. Therefore, they were trying to cast out everything.

I think we have learned that you can't cast out flesh and you can't discipline spirits. If we have sin in our lives or lusts or bad habits, they need to be dealt with, discipline needs to be applied until we overcome, and so on. How-ever, if there truly is a demon, it can't be disciplined or worked out. It has to be cast out.

Simple facts: You repent and turn from sin. You cast out evil spirits. It won't do you any good to cast out that flesh problem of yours or repent of that demon.

We must learn to know the difference between sheep, goats, and wolves and also to recognize hirelings from true shepherds.

●

SHEEP LOVE TO

LIE DOWN

IN GREEN PASTURES

AND DRINK FROM

STILL WATERS.

*

THE HIGHEST COMMODITY

OF SHEEP

IS THE WOOL

THAT THEY GROW.

NO OTHER CREATURE

GROWS IT.

IT COMES NATURALLY

WITH SHEEP.

●

CHAPTER 4
SHEEP

"The Lord is my shepherd; I shall not want.

He maketh me to lie down in green pastures: he leadeth me beside the still waters."

Psalm 23:1-2

This is so true about sheep in their relationship to their shepherd. It is the desire of every good shepherd to lead his sheep in this fashion. It is the desire of sheep to have a shepherd who is capable of providing green pastures and still waters. Sheep love still waters. They do not enjoy fast-moving, agitated waters—in fact, most times won't even draw from them. (This is not always true, however, with goats and wolves.)

In an attempt to apply these truths to our lives, let's bring them into focus by comparison and illustration. Today in our churches we find some believers who love it when they are in peaceful, quiet conditions. These believers do not enjoy turmoil or strife. In fact, if you were to tell them derogatory remarks about another person, they would refuse to listen to you (drink from those waters) even if they were being told it was for "prayer purposes." These are true sheep. They love to drink from still waters. The

less strife, arguing, doctrinal debate, dissension, and turmoil present, the more they enjoy. True sheep will turn
away from agitated waters even if they thirst. They will
wait for the proper drinking conditions. Sheep are a divine
pleasure to pastor!

Sheep also love to lie down in green pastures. This is
a definite sheep-like attitude. Goats do not like to lie down
in green pastures as well as they like to roam. Wolves do
not enjoy green pastures as much as high places.

Green pastures certainly represent fresh and moist
grazing and delicious-looking feeding areas. This is com-
parable to believers entering their local churches to feed
upon the Word of God offered by their pastor.

Sheep never miss a feeding time. They are hungry and
very eager to graze in green pastures. They are not in a
hurry but will stay as long as the shepherd allows them to
eat. Believe it or not, there are Christians who are like this.
They can hardly wait to get to the next church service.
They crave their pastor's teachings. They will come once,
twice, three times a week to feed on the Word of God.
They come in with their utensils—Bibles, notepads, and
pens. They are ready for a luscious meal. They don't place
a time restriction on their shepherd; he has to monitor them
so they don't bloat from overeating! He will actually have
to shoo them away. Yes, I know we are defining a very elite
group of believers here. They are called "sheep"!

You realize, of course, that many other church members fit the following description: once-a-weekers, short
sermon lovers, clock watchers, mind drifters, note passers,
daydreamers, Bible forgetters, non-notetakers . . . I think
you get the message.

True sheep love green pastures. They crave to lie in them daily to feast in new, fresh grass. They enjoy the comfort of a shepherd watching over them. They are in no hurry.

Sheep love to be sheared. They seem to have an inner confidence in their shepherd that he will keep them fit and proper.

I watched a sheep being sheared at the county fair. They brought that fat old sheep out of its pen into the shearing area. He was slow-moving and looked very overweight. As well as they had cared for him, he still looked dirty and stained.

I was amazed as the shearing proceeded. That old sheep became skinny-looking and clean. When they were done and led that sheep back to the others, he leaped and jumped around with great zeal. He became light and easy—frisky, actually.

This is the way true sheep are in our churches today. They love it when shearing time is over. They become frisky. They don't get angry with their shepherd. They aren't stingy with their wool. (Besides, they are going to grow more, and the growing process starts immediately. It comes naturally for them.)

I'm telling you, this is not true with goats and wolves. They hate shearing time (offerings). They cry, bellow, and growl if you try to take what is theirs.

A good shepherd knows that he has to shear his sheep. If he doesn't, they get over-burdened with the growth of wool. Too much wool causes sheep to become vulnerable to the enemies of their well-being. Too much wool makes it easy for wolves' claws to get a hook on them and drag them away. Too much wool causes them to become easily entangled in nearby brush and bushes. They maneuver somewhat slower and don't fit through narrow passages. Too much wool aids in collecting burrs, briars, and the filth of the earth.

I've watched this in believers' lives today. When they are sheared regularly through tithes, offerings, and pledges, they do much better in their Christian service. Too much money and too little shearing cause them to invest in wrong projects and systems (wolves' claws). Too much wool causes them to become fat and sassy, not fitting the straight and narrow way quite so well. Too much wool causes them to become partners to the world. A good shepherd is going to shear the sheep often, and the sheep will be content in offering their wool.

Now don't get growling at me or butting around because of what I just wrote. We've already determined that goats and wolves do not fit these descriptions. We are referring to sheep here.

I tell flocks of believers that wool is the most valuable commodity they have to offer the shepherd outside of their lives.

Every sheep grows wool naturally. Every believer grows finances naturally. He or she goes to work, earns a paycheck, and brings home money. Everyone has some money. Some have a lot; some have a little. No matter what the amount, you will use it and somehow get more. Something or someone somewhere will place a demand on whatever amount you have. You will spend your money and somehow naturally grow more. What a system!

Who or what places the largest demand on *your* wool? Is it your barber, doctor, dentist, auto salesman, realtor, banker, utility company, grocer, clothier, or is it your pastor? "For where your treasure is, there will your heart be also" (Luke 12:34).

I used to be a shy, timid shepherd when it came to shearing time. When I realized that God and His Kingdom have more right to our wool than anyone or anything, I changed. When I realized that fueling or propelling the gospel to the world was a more valuable investment for sheep than anything else in the universe, I changed. When I learned that sheep love to be sheared by their shepherd and have their wool invested in the Kingdom rather than any other investment, I changed.

Believers have a natural way of growing funds in their lives. What a beautiful system God has given us to bring that wool to the shepherd and have it transformed from everyday money to spiritual propulsion, energizing the gospel around the world.

Come on, sheep, and grow that wool! Come on, shepherds, and shear those sheep! Come on, God, and use it to reap this world!

> *"Be thou diligent to know the state of thy flocks, and look well to thy herds."*
>
> Proverbs 27:23

> *"The lambs are for thy clothing, and the goats are the price of the field.*
>
> *And thou shalt have goats' milk enough for thy food, for the food of thy household, and for the maintenance for thy maidens."*
>
> Proverbs 27:26-27

"Who goeth a warfare any time at his own charges? who planteth a vineyard, and eateth not of the fruit thereof? or who feedeth a flock, and eateth not of the milk of the flock?"

1 Corinthians 9:7

This is a word to shepherds. Notice it mentioned flocks (plural) and their herds (plural). Perhaps there is a difference between flocks and herds.

This passage of scripture also mentions sheep and goats. It tells us there is wool taken from sheep and milk from goats.

Goats can be mingled with sheep because they are seldom harmful. However, they normally are quite the agitators. They aren't going to go for that still-water business. They normally are found butting and causing a little turmoil.

●

GOATS ARE NOT SATISFIED

WITH PEACEFUL GRAZING.

IF THERE IS A WAY

OUT OF THE PASTURE,

THEY WILL FIND IT

EVERY TIME.

●

CHAPTER 5
GOATS

We see this in our churches today. There is always a goat or two causing a little undercurrent and dissension. They don't really mean any harm. They just don't seem to know any better. Turmoil, agitation, and orneriness are what they were bred and raised in. It is in their blood.

I like to remind pastors that goats are not wolves. They will not eat the sheep because they are not the meat eaters that wolves are. Many people forget this and think anyone who causes waves must be a wolf in sheep's clothing. Not necessarily.

Goats don't always go for that green-pasture business. They are not satisfied to graze normally with the sheep. They are not satisfied with the pasture that the shepherd selects. They usually want more. They are a little less timid and a little more suspicious than sheep.

Once again we find this to be true with some of our church members. They are not satisfied with the pastor's vision. They want to extend their borders. They aren't satisfied with surface feedings. They want to get to the root of things. If they were permitted to, they would totally destroy the pasture. Now remember, they are harmful to the pasture, not the sheep.

Goats like to roam. They are not at all content sitting under one shepherd or in one pasture. Their suspicion and unrest will drive them to find out what's happening in the neighboring pastures. If there isn't a way, they'll make one.

Goats aren't easy to shepherd, but that doesn't mean they don't need a shepherd. They may not enjoy a pastor's feeding and may want something different, but that doesn't mean they don't need a pastor's teachings and leadership.

I like to encourage pastors to let the goats be goats and not worry about them or get frightened because of them. Remember, they are not wolves, so they really aren't going to hurt the sheep.

Goats are not worthless. The Bible tells us good shepherds that we can milk the goats. That's right! (Read Proverbs 27:23-27 again.) In fact, it almost carries the connotation that we shepherds can do more milking than shearing. It says that shepherds can have the wool for their clothing, but they can take enough goats' milk for the price of their fields, their food, the food of their household, and the nourishment of their staff personnel.

Please excuse the bluntness of the following paragraph, and don't read it if you are immature.

Goats are valuable. Their milk (money) is worth their trouble. The Bible says we can milk them and use it for the kingdom of God. They are roamers. Soon they will leave your flock and fit into another one for a while. When they get there, the shepherd will get all the milk he can. So while they are under your care, milk them as often as you can! Get all the milk you can before they leave.

Remember please that the milk (offerings) is not the

pastor's but is to be used to evanglize the world and build the kingdom of God.

Now don't butt me too hard or growl at me for the last paragraph!

It is very important for sheep to recognize goats as well as pastors, or they will be innocently caught up in the agitation, suspicion, and roaming.

What's the safeguard?

> *"Obey them that have the rule over you, and submit yourselves: for they watch for your souls, as they that must give account, that they may do it with joy, and not with grief: for that is unprofitable for you."*
>
> Hebrews 13:17

●

WOLVES ALWAYS SEEK

HIGH PLACES

SO THEY CAN KEEP

AN EYE ON THEIR PREY.

*

WOLVES ALWAYS

RUN IN A PACK

AND HAVE LITTLE RESPECT

FOR EACH OTHER.

*

WOLVES ARE MEAT EATERS

AND NORMALLY REFUSE

TO GRAZE.

●

CHAPTER 6
WOLVES

"Take heed therefore unto yourselves, and to all the flock, over the which the Holy Ghost hath made you overseers, to feed the church of God, which He hath purchased with His own blood.

For I know this, that after my departing shall grievous wolves enter in among you, not sparing the flock.

Also of your own selves shall men arise, speaking perverse things, to draw away disciples after them."

Acts 20:28-30

Wolves are sort of a breed of their own. They certainly don't conform to others and, most of the time, not even to each other. Not only do they not want to be part of the flock, but the flock doesn't want them around. Not only are they impossible to shepherd, but every shepherd must run them out, protecting the sheep.

Wolves do not care if the waters are still or agitated. They have their eyes on flesh and blood. They love the high places so they can observe their prey and set up their attack. They don't want any responsibility, but they will receive all the authority and positions you give them.

They may show up in sheep's clothing, but it won't

take you long to know they are there. First of all, sheep are frightened by them, so the flock begins to be unsettled and nervous.

Second, signs will follow wolves that will identify them. Here are some of them. Wolves growl and show their teeth. Sheep never do. (Neither do goats.) Wolves are sly and sneaky. They will do their best to stay away from shepherds and cling to the sheep.

Now remember, wolves are meat eaters. They love flesh and blood. In fact, they go from church to church devouring and living on the carnality, strife, and sin that are there.

If you want to expose a wolf, just throw out a slab of fresh meat (carnality). Just reveal a carnal problem or lust problem that is running rampant through the flock. Wolves will jump on it in a minute. In fact, if there is more than one wolf around, they will fight over it.

No one can deny this problem exists in churches today. Jesus also had to deal with this problem in His own ranks (read John 6:60-71). We learn in these scriptures that Jesus had more than 12 disciples. He had many. They followed Him everywhere seeing the great miracles and hearing the truth proclaimed. They looked like a mighty army. However, one day Jesus preached a sermon about the body and blood of the Lamb. They actually thought He was talking about cannibalism. The Bible records that many of them went back and followed Him no more. They were astounded at His teachings.

Today we see many people gathering together, and they have the look of a mighty army marching. But one day the pastor will teach *one* teaching that astonishes them, and away they will go. What a shame! Let's be humble enough to realize that if it happened to Jesus, as great of a leader as He was, it could happen to us.

Jesus asked the remaining 12 disciples if they also would abandon Him. He spoke a heartrending statement: "Have not I chosen you twelve, and one of you is a devil?" That says it all! That's the way it is today in our churches. The church splits, people leave and are scattered, the shepherd looks bad, and out of the few people who stay, normally the troublemaker is still among them.

Let me bring your attention once again to Paul's teaching in Acts 20:28-32. Here the author, Holy Ghost-inspired Luke, records something worth examining.

Paul warned that not only would grievous wolves enter the flock in the pastor's absence but also some of our own men would rise up and cause division. How sad! Not only do we have to look out for wolves, but we have to be watchful for those who appoint themselves as leaders. They will rise up, speaking perverse things and drawing away disciples after themselves.

We see this problem quite often today. It is comforting to know that wolves identify themselves by their attitudes, actions, and living conditions. At best, both shepherd and sheep can pick them out.

". . . sheep hear his voice . . ."

". . . they know not the voice of strangers."

John 10:4-5

●

IF A WATCHDOG

EVER TURNS WOLF,

HE BECOMES DANGEROUS

TO SHEPHERD AND FLOCK

AND THEREFORE

CANNOT BE TRUSTED WITH SHEEP.

●

CHAPTER 7
WATCHDOGS

It wouldn't be fair to deal with such issues as sheep, goats, and wolves without spending a little time on the sheepdogs or guards of the flock.

"The elders which are among you I exhort . . .

Feed the flock of God which is among you, taking the oversight thereof, not by constraint, but willingly; not for filthy lucre, but of a ready mind;

Neither as being lords over God's heritage, but being ensamples to the flock."

1 Peter 5:1-3

For illustration purposes, please allow me to cause a separation here of elders and pastors. Of course, we know that all pastors are in eldership positions, but not all elders are shepherds.

The pastor is the shepherd of the sheep because the Owner of the sheep (God) has appointed him. The pastor, knowing he cannot shepherd the flock himself, appoints watchdogs (elders) on all the outer perimeters of the fold. These sheepdogs (elders, guards, watchmen) are, of course, well-equipped to do their job and are approved by the Owner of the sheep.

It becomes the duty of the watchmen to keep all the sheep in the fold, corral the goats, and keep the wolves out.

The sheep learn to listen to these watchdogs. If they don't, a small reprimand or coercion is instituted such as a stare down or a bark or a nip of the leg. Whatever it takes, these guards are well-trained to keep the sheep safe and totally under the shepherd's protection.

The wolves also begin to have a respect for these watchdogs because they know that they must break their security in order to enter the fold. It is very difficult for a wolf to overcome a sheepdog because the average wolf is cowardly unless he is running in a pack with other wolves.

If a watchdog (elder) ever turns wolf, he becomes dangerous to the shepherd and the flock and therefore cannot be trusted with the sheep. Once a sheepdog gets the taste of sheeps' blood and meat, he hungers after them and becomes wolfish in his motives. The shepherd needs to be rid of him and notify other shepherds of his change of nature. Otherwise, he will be taken in by other shepherds as a trustworthy watchdog, soon devouring their flock, unsuspected by the pastor.

Now, don't any of you elders growl at me for writing this. Good watchdogs don't turn on shepherds, only wolves do.

This does bring up another very interesting subject. The watchdogs (elders) are strategically positioned on the perimeters of the flock to keep the sheep in and the enemy out. Everyone knows this. They are not to guard the sheep from the shepherd. Never are they positioned between the shepherd and the flock. This positioning would be wolfish not godly.

Elders have not been positioned to watch the pastorate or to keep the pastor from the sheep or the sheep from their pastor.

Elders never turn on their shepherd, who appointed them to their position, unless they have obtained a taste for "lamb chops."

Almost everyone, at one time or another, has driven along viewing the scenery and has come across a flock of sheep in a pasture. Wouldn't it be something if you stopped to watch these sheep graze peacefully and, as you did, your eye caught some extra activity on the hillside? As you looked closer, you saw the shepherd boy leaping, running, and kicking his legs behind him. You noticed that he was trying desperately to free his legs and feet from something trying to devour them. As you observed and things became more clear, you could see that the watchdogs had left their positions and were snapping at the feet of the shepherd. Ha, ha—what a silly-looking sight!

I'm ashamed to tell you this, but this is what I see all over our nation. Many churches are being destroyed by wolves, split by goats, and unguarded because the sheep-dogs (elders) have gotten the taste for sheep. They want their own positions or have become overconcerned for the sheep and left their positions to nip at the shepherd's feet. Shame! Shame!

Now, don't be growling at me!

CHAPTER 8
"THE QUIZ"

Let me draw your attention to a few statements I made in the introductory remarks of this book. The intention of the author is to enlighten church members, not anger them.

It is the desire of the author to better equip pastors to handle hard situations in their folds.

I also stated that each reader would be quizzed as they read the truths on these pages. I pray that I have provoked you to examine your heart with humility, as that is what the Spirit of the Lord instructed me to accomplish.

Would you please take a few honest and holy minutes to finish this book. This portion of the book I have entitled "The Quiz."

This quiz is designed for every believer to examine his or her heart, actions, and servanthood to our Lord Jesus Christ. Please be fair to consider these questions privately and answer them accurately.

Now, I know that everyone *wants* to be a good little lamb. But I also know that not every Christian is. If you have been running with the goats, you probably have picked up some habits of roaming, agitating, and living loosely. If you have been running with wolves, you probably are frightened, hurt, and confused, and maybe you have even started to growl, smell, and act like the pack.

Please know that you can always improve your relationship with the Lord, your pastor, and the flock. As you take this self-quiz, admit where you fall short of being a good little sheep, and go to work at improving your character and performance.

Now, please let me pray for you before you begin.

"Father, I pray for these readers, that they will be strong enough to overcome their opinions of this book and their hurts, prejudices, angers, anxieties, and pride so that they can properly evaluate (judge) themselves. Please, Lord, encourage them to be confident that You will help them change to the better. You, Sir, already know what and who they are. You, Sir, already know how they have been behaving in the house of the Lord. I pray, Heavenly Father, that all of us would become good sheep in Your fold, protected by good elders, and shepherded by good pastors."

"But let a man examine himself . . .

For if we would judge ourselves, we should not be judged."

1 Corinthians 11:28, 31

". . . That thou mayest know how thou oughtest to behave thyself in the house of God, which is the church of the Living God . . ."

1 Timothy 3:15

THE QUIZ

Question #1

Do you want to be a sheep—pure, holy, humble, submitted, and fitted into the fold?

Question #2

Are you a sheep or do you have sheep-like attributes?

A.   Do you hate strife, envy, malice, dissension, arguing, or doctrinal debates?

B.   Do you enjoy still waters (submitting to your pastor)?

C.   Do you love to go to church every service?

D.   Do you love to listen to the Word preached?

E.   Do you hunger after truth from the Word?

F.   Do you forget about the length of time you are in church?

G.   Do you not care how long your pastor preaches?

H.   Do you love to be sheared?

I.   Do you love to have more than one offering per service?

J.   Do you love to plant your treasure in the Kingdom?

K.   Do you receive admonition and correction from your pastor easily?

L.   Are you content where you are in the flock?

Question #3

Are you a goat or do you have goatish attributes?

A.   Do you agitate others in the flock?

B.   Do you always find yourself gossiping?

C.   Do other agitators draw to you easily?

D. Do you always have to get to the root of every problem in your church?

E. Do you have urges to leave your church?

F. Do you fight feelings of disagreement or resentment toward your pastor?

G. Do you have trouble making it to every service?

H. Do you find it a real discipline to listen to the Word for long lengths of time?

I. Does it make you suspicious when you don't know all the facts about other churches and meetings?

J. Do you have trouble sitting under one pastor and being content to be part of only one church?

K. Are you always butting the system and fighting a way out of the flock (exempting yourself)?

L. Do you have trouble when you are admonished or corrected by church leaders?

Question #4

Are you a wolf or do you have wolfish attributes?

A. Are you always feeling an inward drive to have a chief seat or high position in the church?

B. Do you find yourself bothered if you have to do what others are doing in the flock?

C. Are you drawn into strife and carnal things easily?

D. Have you been in trouble with church leadership and unable to work it out?

E. Do you have problems submitting to your pastor—inwardly?

F. Do offerings and talk of money in the church anger you or cause you resentment?

G. Are you ever trying to defame your pastor's teachings and drawing disciples after yourself?

H. Do you defame or talk negatively about your pastor, the church, or others when you are in a group?

I. Do you have a lack of hunger for the things of God?

J. Have you become sly, sneaky, and deceitful in your attitude and actions?

K. Do you gather security from people who support your views?

L. How many churches and pastors have you had in the past five years, and do you have one now?

Question #5

Are you a good, trustworthy elder, or have you become wolfish in your performance and attitudes?

A. Do you easily receive instruction from your pastor?

B. Do you keep the sheep in the fold, or do you allow areas for them to leave?

C. Do you watch outwardly for wolves, or do you turn on your pastor?

D. Do you judge your pastor for the way he shepherds the flock?

E. Whose side are you mostly on—pastor's, sheep's, yours, enemy's, or situation's?

F. Have you acquired a taste for sheep, and do you plan to someday have your own flock?

G. Are you always placing yourself between your pastor and the sheep?

H. Do you ever get overconcerned for the people and have to fight feeling sympathy toward them?

I. Are you serving the Lord, or are you inwardly hoping for money, prestige, or position from the sheepfold?

J. Do you get angry at God's people and treat them with verbal or physical abuse?

K. Is your pastor always having to remind you to keep your nose where it belongs and out of the decision-making of the pastorate?

L. Are you keeping a list of all of your pastor's sins, problems, and shortcomings to try to build a case against him, proving he is unsuitable for his job or scripturally unfair to the flock?

Question #6

Are you a good shepherd, or have you picked up some traces of a hireling?

A. Do you love your appointment to pastor?

B. Do you love and respect the sheep?

C. Do you teach them and build them up?

D. Are you afraid to shear your sheep?

E. Are you afraid of goats causing agitation in your flock?

F. Do you run from problems, or do you confront them?

G. Are you hard and not easily approached?

H. Do you always put the blame on others?

I. Do you constantly "consider the state of your flocks and the condition of your herd"?

J. Do you try to protect your reputation when trouble comes to your flock?

K. Are you fearful of troublemakers?

L. Are you afraid of people who oppose you?

ANSWER SHEET

Question #1

Do you want to be a sheep?   Yes

Question #2

Are you a sheep?

A.	Yes	G.	I do not
B.	Yes	H.	Yes
C.	Yes	I.	Yes
D.	Yes	J.	Yes
E.	Yes	K.	Yes
F.	Yes	L.	Yes

If you answered all "yes," you are a good sheep.

Question #3

Are you a goat?

A.	Yes	G.	Yes
B.	Yes	H.	Yes
C.	Yes	I.	Yes
D.	Yes	J.	Yes
E.	Yes	K.	Yes
F.	Yes	L.	Yes

If you answered more than four questions with a "yes," you are too goatish. Ask God to help you change—AND consult your pastor immediately!

Question #4

Are you a wolf?

A.	Yes	G.	Yes
B.	Yes	H.	Yes
C.	Yes	I.	Yes
D.	Yes	J.	Yes
E.	Yes	K.	Yes
F.	Yes	L.	Two or more/ None

If you answered more than four of these "yes," you are too wolfish. REPENT, and ask God to help you. Seek pastoral help immediately.

Question #5

Are you a good elder?

A.	Yes	G.	No
B.	In the fold	H.	No
C.	Watch outwardly	I.	Serving the Lord
D.	No	J.	No
E.	No	K.	No
F.	No	L.	No

If you got more than two of these wrong, you need to get help before you hurt someone permanently. Ask your pastor for an evaluation of yourself, and resign for a season if need be.

Question #6

Are you a shepherd or a hireling?

A.	Yes	G.	No
B.	Yes	H.	No
C.	Yes	I.	Yes
D.	No	J.	No
E.	No	K.	No
F.	Confront them	L.	No

If you answered two or more of these wrong, you should really evaluate what it is that you are doing and why you are doing it. Fast and pray to break all signs of a hireling in your life.

●

IF YOU ARE A SHEEP,

BUT YOU HAVE ATTRIBUTES

OR HABITS THAT ARE

WOLFISH OR GOATISH,

YOU CAN CHANGE!

YOUR SHEPHERD

CAN HELP YOU.

LET HIM.

●

CHAPTER 9
MAKING THE CHANGE

Examining yourself and humbly admitting where you fall short are the first steps to changing and improving your life.

If your problems, attitudes, characteristics, and performance are severely different than what you know is right, then call a fast for yourself and pray. God will honor you and help you. Following is a list of benefits that come to us when we fast and pray God's way (taken from Isaiah 58:6-11).

1. Bands of wickedness loosed
2. Heavy burdens undone
3. Freed from opposition
4. Every yoke broken
5. Light breaks forth in the morning
6. Your health springs forth speedily
7. Your righteousness shall go before you
8. The glory of the Lord shall be your rear guard
9. Your prayers shall be answered
10. The Lord shall guide you continually

It's amazing how easy it is to discipline our actions and improve our performance once we've gotten our hearts right, our motives godly, and our attitudes lined up with the Scriptures. I felt led of the Lord to put a list of Bible guidelines before you that, if obeyed and practiced, would cause you (as believers) to be obedient sheep and very productive in the Kingdom. Please take time to read them and place them as stepping stones in your path.

1 Corinthians 14:26

Be sure your motivation is always to build up the entire Body. (This includes your pastor.)

2 Corinthians 10:12-15

Stop comparing yourself with others and their positions, appointments, gifts, and achievements. Do what God wants *you* to do.

1 Thessalonians 4:11

Try to be quiet, mind your own business, and keep your hands busy in the Kingdom.

Luke 3:13-14

Do your own work, and be content with the results and rewards of it.

James 4:6-8

Work hard at staying humble, and God will never resist you but will always apply grace to your life.

1 Timothy 4:11-16

Study your Bible so you will be ready and equipped whenever God wants to use you.

1 John 1:9

Keep your heart right, confess your sin, and keep your avenues to God open.

Hebrews 10:23-25

Fellowship and commune with those who are doing things right and holy.

1 Thessalonians 5:12-13

Keep your view of leadership sweet and clean, and be sure you are responding biblically.

Malachi 3:10, Hebrews 7:5-8

Go to church, and present your tithes and offerings.

So often today we hear people saying that God showed them something, God told them something, God led them to do something, God revealed something to them, and so on.

Of course, we know God is speaking to mankind today, and He is showing, telling, and revealing things to His people and leading them. Thank God that He is! However, it is also plain to see that many people are hearing voices, dreaming dreams, seeing visions, and getting leadings from sources other than God. The result of course is that people are doing things that are destructive to the family of God, but they can't see it because of their conviction that God led them to do it.

To help believers sort out some of this confusion and to be sure they are being led by the Spirit of God, I have included in this book a small plan. Look it over and adapt to it. It will certainly help to keep your vessel on course.

1. You do have the ability to hear from God!

"My sheep hear my voice, and I know them, and they follow me . . ."

John 10:27

"Bind them continually upon thine heart, and tie them about thy neck.

When thou goest, it shall lead thee; when thou sleepest, it shall keep thee; and when thou awakest, it shall talk with thee."

Proverbs 6:21-22

2. Do you know the plan of God?

"Behold, I will do a new thing; now it shall spring forth; shall ye not know it? I will even make a way in the wilderness, and rivers in the desert."

Isaiah 43:19

God will not trick you or play with your life as though you were a puppet. "He just wanted to see if I would do it." This statement does not fit the God we serve. It is a fable!

3. Do you know the will of God?

"I beseech you therefore, brethren, by the mercies of God, that ye present your bodies a living sacrifice, holy, acceptable unto God, which is your reasonable service.

And be not conformed to this world: but be ye transformed by the renewing of your mind, that ye may prove what is that good, and acceptable, and perfect, will of God."

Romans 12:1-2

God reveals it on a daily basis—line upon line, precept upon precept. If you only show up when you want information, you're going to be disappointed.

4.   Do you know the timing of God?

"Cast not away therefore your confidence, which hath great recompence of reward.

For ye have need of patience, that, after ye have done the will of God, ye might receive the promise."

Hebrews 10:35-36

"To every thing there is a season, and a time to every purpose under the heaven:

A time to be born, and a time to die; a time to plant, and a time to pluck up that which is planted;

A time to kill, and a time to heal; a time to break down, and a time to build up;

A time to weep, and a time to laugh; a time to mourn, and a time to dance;

A time to cast away stones, and a time to gather stones together; a time to embrace, and a time to refrain from embracing;

A time to get, and a time to lose; a time to keep, and a time to cast away;

A time to rend, and a time to sew; a time to keep silence, and a time to speak;

A time to love, and a time to hate; a time of war, and a time of peace.

What profit hath he that worketh in that wherein he laboureth?

I have seen the travail, which God hath given to the sons of men to be exercised in it.

He hath made every thing beautiful in his time: also he hath set the world in their heart, so that no man can find out the work that God maketh from the beginning to the end."

Ecclesiastes 3:1-11

5. Where does prophecy fit in?

"This charge I commit unto thee, son Timothy, according to the prophecies which went before on thee, that thou by them mightest war a good warfare . . ."

1 Timothy 1:18

Prophecy can be God's map in our lives. But first of all, let's remember we are led by the Spirit of God (Rom. 8:14), not by a prophet of God.

Prophecy may fail.

"Charity never faileth: but whether there be prophecies, they shall fail; whether there be tongues, they shall cease; whether there be knowledge, it shall vanish away."

1 Corinthians 13:8

We only know in part.

"For we know in part, and we prophesy in part."

1 Corinthians 13:9

6. What about confirmations?

"This is the third time I am coming to you. In the mouth of two or three witnesses shall every word be established."

2 Corinthians 13:1

If you need confirmations, wait for them. If you don't need them, what are you waiting for?

"Three witnesses" doesn't always mean three different vessels. Paul, being the same vessel, witnessed three different times to establish something here to the Corinthians.

7.   Do I have leadership approval?

"Obey them that have the rule over you, and submit yourselves: for they watch for your souls, as they that must give account, that they may do it with joy, and not with grief: for that is unprofitable for you."

Hebrews 13:17

CHAPTER 10
TIMES OF DISAGREEMENT

When two or more people come together, there are differences of opinions, ideas, and convictions. If we freely voice and follow these leadings, then we will automatically place ourselves in a position of disagreement and division.

We do understand, however, that it is not a sin to have your own ideas, opinions, and convictions. How we communicate these and how they motivate us to perform are what we become scripturally and socially responsible for.

I have included here a biblical list of principles that will guide you and keep you scripturally and socially right even when you disagree with your leaders.

1. These three responses always come when the Word of Christ is delivered. Be one who believes.

    a. Some mock.

    b. Some procrastinate.

    c. Some believe and cleave to the preacher.

"And when they heard of the resurrection of the dead, some mocked: and others said, We will hear thee again of this matter.

So Paul departed from among them.

Howbeit certain men clave unto him, and believed: among the which was Dionysius the Areopagite, and a woman named Damaris, and others with them."

Acts 17:32-34

2.   Always treat your leaders this way, and you will always be right with God.

    a.   Do them no harm.

"Saying, Touch not mine anointed, and do my prophets no harm."

Psalm 105:15

    b.   Esteem them highly in love.

"And we beseech you, brethren, to know them which labour among you, and are over you in the Lord, and admonish you;

And to esteem them very highly in love for their work's sake. And be at peace among yourselves."

1 Thessalonians 5:12-13

3.   Stay submitted.

"Obey them that have the rule over you, and submit yourselves: for they watch for your souls, as they that must give account, that they may do it with joy, and not with grief: for that is unprofitable for you."

Hebrews 13:17

4.   Do not get out of Bible order.

"Rebuke not an elder, but intreat him as a father; and the younger men as brethren . . ."

1 Timothy 5:1

5. Keep all things edifying and joyful.

"And certain men which came down from Judaea taught the brethren, and said, Except ye be circumcised after the manner of Moses, ye cannot be saved.

When therefore Paul and Barnabas had no small dissension and disputation with them, they determined that Paul and Barnabas, and certain other of them, should go up to Jerusalem unto the apostles and elders about this question.

And being brought on their way by the church, they passed through Phenice and Samaria, declaring the conversion of the Gentiles: and they caused great joy unto all the brethren.

And when they were come to Jerusalem, they were received of the church, and of the apostles and elders, and they declared all things that God had done with them.

But there rose up certain of the sect of the Pharisees which believed, saying, That it was needful to circumcise them, and to command them to keep the law of Moses.

And the apostles and elders came together for to consider of this matter.

And when there had been much disputing, Peter rose up, and said unto them, Men and brethren, ye know how that a good while ago God made choice among us, that the Gentiles by my mouth should hear the word of the gospel, and believe."

Acts 15:1-7

6. Pray for your leaders.

"Finally, brethren, pray for us, that the word of the

Lord may have free course, and be glorified, even as it is with you . . ."

2 Thessalonians 3:1

7.   Study your Bible openly.

"And the brethren immediately sent away Paul and Silas by night unto Berea: who coming thither went into the synagogue of the Jews.

These were more noble than those in Thessalonica, in that they received the word with all readiness of mind, and searched the scriptures daily, whether those things were so."

Acts 17:10-11

8.   Don't spread your feelings.

"Take heed therefore unto yourselves, and to all the flock, over the which the Holy Ghost hath made you overseers, to feed the church of God, which he hath purchased with his own blood."

Acts 20:28

PRAYER OF SALVATION

YOU CAN BE SAVED FROM ETERNAL DAMNATION and get God's help now in this life. All you have to do is humble your heart, believe in Christ's work at Calvary for you, and pray the prayer below.

"Dear Heavenly Father:

I know that I have sinned and fallen short of Your expectations of me. I have come to realize that I cannot run my own life. I do not want to continue the way I've been living, neither do I want to face an eternity of torment and damnation.

I know that the wages of sin is death, but I can be spared from this through the gift of the Lord Jesus Christ. I believe that He died for me, and I receive His provision now. I will not be ashamed of Him, and I will tell all my friends and family members that I have made this wonderful decision.

Dear Lord Jesus:

Come into my heart now and live in me and be my Savior, Master, and Lord. I will do my very best to chase after You and to learn Your ways by submitting to a pastor, reading my Bible, going to a church that preaches about **You**, and keeping sin out of my life.

I also ask You to give me the power to be healed from any sickness and disease and to deliver me from those things that have me bound.

I love You and thank You for having me, and I am eagerly looking forward to a long, beautiful relationship with You."

Books by Mark T. Barclay

Beware of Seducing Spirits

This is not a book on demonology. It is a book about the misbehavior of men and women and the seducing/deceiving spirits that influence them to do what they do. Brother Barclay exposes the most prominent seducing spirits of the last days.

Beware of the Sin of Familiarity

This book is a scriptural study on the most devastating sin in the body of Christ today. The truths in this book will make you aware of this excess familiarity and reveal to you some counterattacks.

Building a Supernatural Church

A guide to pioneering, organizing, and establishing a new local church. This is a fast-reading, simple, instructional guide to leaders and helps people who are working together to build the Church.

Charging the Year 2000

This book will remind you of the last-days' promises of God as well as alert you to the many snares and falsehoods with which Satan will try to deceive and seduce last-days' believers. "A handbook for living in the '90s."

Enduring Hardness

God has called His Church an army and the believers, soldiers. It is mandatory that all Christians endure hardness as good soldiers of Jesus Christ. This book will help build more backbone in you.

How to Avoid Shipwreck

A book of preventive medicine, helping people stay strong and full of faith. You will be strengthened by this book as you learn how to anchor your soul.

How to Relate to Your Pastor

It is very important in these last days that God's people understand the office of pastor. As we put into practice these principles, the Church will grow in numbers and also increase its vision for the world.

How to Always Reap a Harvest

In this book Brother Barclay explains the principles that make believers successful and fruitful. It shows you how to live a better life and become far more productive and enjoy a full harvest.

Improving Your Performance

Every Christian everywhere needs to read this book. Even leaders will be challenged by this writing. It will help tremendously in the organization and unity of your ministry and working force.

The Making of a Man of God
In this book you'll find some of the greatest, yet simplest, insights to becoming a man or woman of God and to launching your ministry with accuracy and credibility. The longevity of your ministry will be enhanced by the truths herein. You will learn the difference between being a convert, an epistle, a disciple, and a minister.

Preachers of Righteousness
This is not a book for pulpiteers or reverends only but for all of us. It reveals the real ministry style of Jesus Christ and the sold-out commitment of His followers—the most powerful, awesome force on the face of the earth.

The Real Truth About Tithing
With the extremely fast lifestyles of these last days, it leaves little time to thoroughly study God's Word. When you finish this book, you will be fully equipped and informed to tithe properly and accurately. All of your tithing questions should be answered. Your life will never be the same.

The Remnant Church
God has always had a people and will always have a people. Brother Barclay speaks of the upcoming revival and how we can be those who are alive and remain when our Master returns.

Sheep, Goats, Wolves
A scriptural yet practical explanation of human behavior in our local churches and how church leaders and members can deal with each other. You will especially enjoy the tests that are in the back of this book.

The Sin of Lawlessness
Lawlessness always challenges authority and ultimately is designed to hurt people. This book will convict those who are in lawlessness and warn those who could be future victims. It will help your life and straighten your walk with Him.

Basic Christian Handbook (minibook)
This book contains basic doctrines that are simple yet necessary to every Christian's walk with God. It will be a vital help to new converts in the Kingdom. This also makes a great tract or altar counselor's tool.

The Captain's Mantle (minibook)
Something happened in the cave Adullum. Find out how 400 distressed, indebted, and discontented men came out of that cave as one of the most awesome armies in history.